50 Quick Fix Vegan Recipes for Home

By: Kelly Johnson

Table of Contents

- One-Pot Vegetable Pasta
- Chickpea Salad Sandwich
- Quick Vegan Chili
- Zucchini Noodles with Pesto
- Avocado Toast with Tomato
- Stir-Fried Tofu and Broccoli
- Spinach and Lentil Soup
- Vegan Quesadillas
- Sweet Potato and Black Bean Tacos
- Curried Chickpea Bowl
- Easy Vegetable Fried Rice
- Creamy Avocado Pasta
- Mediterranean Quinoa Salad
- Cauliflower Tacos with Lime
- Peanut Butter Banana Smoothie
- No-Cook Cucumber Sushi
- Simple Veggie Stir-Fry
- Hummus and Veggie Wraps
- Quick Vegan Pizza
- Lentil and Quinoa Salad
- Raw Veggie Spring Rolls
- Tomato Basil Gazpacho
- Banana Oatmeal Cookies
- Chickpea and Spinach Stew
- Vegan Tofu Scramble
- Black Bean and Corn Salad
- Smashed Chickpea Salad
- Quick Vegetable Curry
- Pasta Salad with Cherry Tomatoes
- Sweet Potato and Kale Hash
- Spinach and Mushroom Wraps
- Berry Smoothie Bowl
- Grilled Vegetable Sandwich
- Quinoa and Black Bean Burgers
- Spicy Sriracha Chickpeas

- Cabbage and Carrot Slaw
- Vegan Cauliflower Buffalo Wings
- Almond Butter Energy Bites
- Simple Vegan Chili Rellenos
- Rice and Bean Bowl
- Zesty Lemon Couscous Salad
- Chickpea and Avocado Dip
- Vegan Burrito Bowl
- Coconut Curry Noodles
- Cucumber and Avocado Salad
- Quick Veggie Tacos
- Lemon Garlic Quinoa
- Sweet Potato and Chickpea Buddha Bowl
- Vegan Apple Crisp
- No-Bake Chocolate Energy Bars

One-Pot Vegetable Pasta

Ingredients

- 8 oz pasta (your choice)
- 2 cups mixed vegetables (bell peppers, zucchini, spinach)
- 3 cups vegetable broth
- 2 cloves garlic, minced
- 1 teaspoon Italian seasoning
- Salt and pepper, to taste
- Olive oil, for drizzling

Instructions

1. **Combine Ingredients:**
   - In a large pot, combine pasta, mixed vegetables, vegetable broth, garlic, Italian seasoning, salt, and pepper.
2. **Cook:**
   - Bring to a boil over medium-high heat. Reduce heat and simmer for 10-12 minutes, stirring occasionally, until pasta is cooked and liquid is mostly absorbed.
3. **Serve:**
   - Drizzle with olive oil and enjoy!

Chickpea Salad Sandwich

Ingredients

- 1 can chickpeas, drained and rinsed
- 1/4 cup vegan mayonnaise
- 1 tablespoon Dijon mustard
- 1/4 cup celery, chopped
- 1/4 cup red onion, chopped
- Salt and pepper, to taste
- Bread or wraps for serving

Instructions

1. **Mash Chickpeas:**
   - In a bowl, mash chickpeas with a fork until chunky.
2. **Mix Ingredients:**
   - Stir in vegan mayonnaise, Dijon mustard, celery, red onion, salt, and pepper until well combined.
3. **Serve:**
   - Spread on bread or wraps and enjoy!

Quick Vegan Chili

Ingredients

- 1 can black beans, drained and rinsed
- 1 can kidney beans, drained and rinsed
- 1 can diced tomatoes
- 1 cup corn (frozen or canned)
- 1 onion, chopped
- 2 cloves garlic, minced
- 2 tablespoons chili powder
- Salt and pepper, to taste

Instructions

1. **Sauté Onion and Garlic:**
   - In a pot, sauté onion and garlic until soft.
2. **Add Remaining Ingredients:**
   - Add black beans, kidney beans, diced tomatoes, corn, chili powder, salt, and pepper. Stir to combine.
3. **Cook:**
   - Simmer for 15-20 minutes, stirring occasionally.
4. **Serve:**
   - Enjoy hot, garnished with your favorite toppings!

Zucchini Noodles with Pesto

Ingredients

- 2 medium zucchinis, spiralized
- 1/2 cup basil pesto (store-bought or homemade)
- 1 tablespoon olive oil
- Salt and pepper, to taste
- Cherry tomatoes, halved (optional)

Instructions

1. **Sauté Zoodles:**
   - In a pan, heat olive oil over medium heat. Add zucchini noodles and sauté for 2-3 minutes until slightly tender.
2. **Add Pesto:**
   - Stir in pesto and cook for another minute. Season with salt and pepper.
3. **Serve:**
   - Top with cherry tomatoes if desired and enjoy!

Avocado Toast with Tomato

Ingredients

- 2 slices whole-grain bread
- 1 ripe avocado
- 1 medium tomato, sliced
- Salt and pepper, to taste
- Red pepper flakes (optional)

Instructions

1. **Toast Bread:**
    - Toast the slices of bread until golden brown.
2. **Mash Avocado:**
    - In a bowl, mash the avocado with a fork. Season with salt and pepper.
3. **Assemble:**
    - Spread mashed avocado on toasted bread and top with tomato slices.
4. **Serve:**
    - Sprinkle with red pepper flakes if desired and enjoy!

Stir-Fried Tofu and Broccoli

Ingredients

- 1 block firm tofu, drained and cubed
- 2 cups broccoli florets
- 2 tablespoons soy sauce
- 1 tablespoon sesame oil
- 2 cloves garlic, minced
- 1 teaspoon ginger, minced
- Sesame seeds, for garnish

Instructions

1. **Sauté Tofu:**
    - In a pan, heat sesame oil over medium heat. Add tofu cubes and sauté until golden brown.
2. **Add Vegetables:**
    - Add broccoli, garlic, and ginger. Stir-fry for about 5 minutes until broccoli is tender-crisp.
3. **Add Soy Sauce:**
    - Pour in soy sauce and stir to coat everything.
4. **Serve:**
    - Garnish with sesame seeds and enjoy!

Spinach and Lentil Soup

Ingredients

- 1 cup lentils (green or brown), rinsed
- 4 cups vegetable broth
- 2 cups fresh spinach, chopped
- 1 onion, chopped
- 2 carrots, diced
- 2 cloves garlic, minced
- 1 teaspoon thyme
- Salt and pepper, to taste

Instructions

1. **Sauté Vegetables:**
   - In a pot, sauté onion, carrots, and garlic until softened.
2. **Add Lentils and Broth:**
   - Stir in lentils, vegetable broth, thyme, salt, and pepper. Bring to a boil.
3. **Simmer:**
   - Reduce heat and simmer for about 25-30 minutes until lentils are tender.
4. **Add Spinach:**
   - Stir in spinach and cook for another 5 minutes.
5. **Serve:**
   - Enjoy hot, seasoned to taste!

Enjoy your delicious and wholesome meals!

Vegan Quesadillas

Ingredients

- 4 whole wheat tortillas
- 1 can black beans, drained and rinsed
- 1 cup corn (fresh or frozen)
- 1 red bell pepper, diced
- 1 teaspoon cumin
- Salt and pepper, to taste
- 1 cup vegan cheese (optional)
- Salsa and avocado, for serving

Instructions

1. **Prepare Filling:**
   - In a bowl, combine black beans, corn, bell pepper, cumin, salt, and pepper.
2. **Assemble Quesadillas:**
   - On one half of each tortilla, add the filling and top with vegan cheese if using. Fold the tortilla over.
3. **Cook:**
   - Heat a skillet over medium heat and cook each quesadilla for 3-4 minutes on each side until golden and crispy.
4. **Serve:**
   - Slice and serve with salsa and avocado!

Sweet Potato and Black Bean Tacos

Ingredients

- 2 medium sweet potatoes, peeled and diced
- 1 can black beans, drained and rinsed
- 1 teaspoon chili powder
- 1 teaspoon cumin
- Salt and pepper, to taste
- Corn tortillas
- Avocado and cilantro, for topping

Instructions

1. **Roast Sweet Potatoes:**
   - Preheat oven to 400°F (200°C). Toss sweet potatoes with chili powder, cumin, salt, and pepper. Spread on a baking sheet and roast for 25-30 minutes.
2. **Warm Black Beans:**
   - In a saucepan, heat black beans over low heat until warmed through.
3. **Assemble Tacos:**
   - Warm corn tortillas and fill with roasted sweet potatoes and black beans.
4. **Serve:**
   - Top with avocado and cilantro!

Curried Chickpea Bowl

Ingredients

- 1 can chickpeas, drained and rinsed
- 1 cup cooked quinoa or rice
- 1 can coconut milk
- 1 tablespoon curry powder
- 2 cups spinach
- Salt and pepper, to taste

Instructions

1. **Cook Chickpeas:**
    - In a saucepan, combine chickpeas, coconut milk, curry powder, salt, and pepper. Simmer for 10 minutes.
2. **Add Spinach:**
    - Stir in spinach and cook until wilted.
3. **Serve:**
    - Serve over cooked quinoa or rice in bowls!

Easy Vegetable Fried Rice

Ingredients

- 2 cups cooked rice (preferably day-old)
- 1 cup mixed vegetables (carrots, peas, bell peppers)
- 2 tablespoons soy sauce
- 2 cloves garlic, minced
- 1 tablespoon sesame oil
- Green onions, for garnish

Instructions

1. **Heat Oil:**
    - In a large skillet, heat sesame oil over medium heat. Add garlic and mixed vegetables, and sauté for 3-4 minutes.
2. **Add Rice:**
    - Stir in cooked rice and soy sauce. Cook for an additional 5 minutes, stirring frequently.
3. **Serve:**
    - Garnish with green onions and enjoy!

Creamy Avocado Pasta

Ingredients

- 8 oz pasta (your choice)
- 1 ripe avocado
- 2 tablespoons lemon juice
- 2 cloves garlic
- Salt and pepper, to taste
- Cherry tomatoes, for topping

Instructions

1. **Cook Pasta:**
    - Cook pasta according to package instructions. Drain and set aside.
2. **Make Sauce:**
    - In a blender, combine avocado, lemon juice, garlic, salt, and pepper. Blend until smooth.
3. **Combine:**
    - Toss the pasta with the creamy avocado sauce.
4. **Serve:**
    - Top with cherry tomatoes and enjoy!

Mediterranean Quinoa Salad

Ingredients

- 1 cup quinoa, cooked
- 1 cup cherry tomatoes, halved
- 1 cucumber, diced
- 1/4 red onion, diced
- 1/4 cup olives, sliced
- 1/4 cup parsley, chopped
- Juice of 1 lemon
- Salt and pepper, to taste

Instructions

1. **Combine Ingredients:**
    - In a large bowl, mix cooked quinoa, cherry tomatoes, cucumber, red onion, olives, and parsley.
2. **Dress Salad:**
    - Drizzle with lemon juice and season with salt and pepper. Toss to combine.
3. **Serve:**
    - Enjoy chilled or at room temperature!

Cauliflower Tacos with Lime

Ingredients

- 1 small head cauliflower, cut into florets
- 2 tablespoons olive oil
- 1 teaspoon cumin
- 1 teaspoon chili powder
- Salt and pepper, to taste
- Corn tortillas
- Lime wedges, for serving

Instructions

1. **Roast Cauliflower:**
    - Preheat oven to 425°F (220°C). Toss cauliflower with olive oil, cumin, chili powder, salt, and pepper. Spread on a baking sheet and roast for 20-25 minutes.
2. **Warm Tortillas:**
    - Warm corn tortillas in a skillet.
3. **Assemble Tacos:**
    - Fill tortillas with roasted cauliflower and squeeze lime juice over the top.
4. **Serve:**
    - Enjoy fresh!

Peanut Butter Banana Smoothie

Ingredients

- 1 banana
- 1 tablespoon peanut butter
- 1 cup almond milk (or any plant-based milk)
- 1 tablespoon chia seeds (optional)
- Ice cubes (optional)

Instructions

1. **Blend Ingredients:**
   - In a blender, combine banana, peanut butter, almond milk, chia seeds, and ice if desired. Blend until smooth.
2. **Serve:**
   - Pour into a glass and enjoy immediately!

Enjoy your delicious and healthy meals!

No-Cook Cucumber Sushi

Ingredients

- 1 large cucumber
- 1/2 cup cooked quinoa or rice
- 1 carrot, julienned
- 1 bell pepper, thinly sliced
- 1 avocado, sliced
- Soy sauce or tamari, for dipping

Instructions

1. **Prepare Cucumber:**
    - Slice the cucumber in half lengthwise and scoop out the seeds with a spoon.
2. **Fill Cucumber:**
    - Stuff the cucumber halves with quinoa or rice, carrot, bell pepper, and avocado.
3. **Slice:**
    - Cut into bite-sized pieces and serve with soy sauce or tamari for dipping.

Simple Veggie Stir-Fry

Ingredients

- 2 cups mixed vegetables (broccoli, bell peppers, snap peas)
- 1 tablespoon soy sauce
- 1 tablespoon sesame oil
- 2 cloves garlic, minced
- 1 teaspoon ginger, minced
- Cooked rice or quinoa, for serving

Instructions

1. **Heat Oil:**
    - In a skillet, heat sesame oil over medium heat. Add garlic and ginger, sauté for 1 minute.
2. **Add Vegetables:**
    - Add mixed vegetables and stir-fry for 5-7 minutes until tender-crisp.
3. **Season:**
    - Stir in soy sauce and cook for an additional minute.
4. **Serve:**
    - Serve over cooked rice or quinoa.

Hummus and Veggie Wraps

Ingredients

- 4 whole grain tortillas
- 1 cup hummus
- 1 cup mixed vegetables (carrots, bell peppers, spinach)
- Salt and pepper, to taste

Instructions

1. **Spread Hummus:**
    - Spread hummus evenly over each tortilla.
2. **Add Veggies:**
    - Layer mixed vegetables on top, seasoning with salt and pepper.
3. **Wrap:**
    - Roll up each tortilla tightly and slice in half.
4. **Serve:**
    - Enjoy as a quick lunch or snack!

Quick Vegan Pizza

Ingredients

- 1 pre-made pizza crust (whole grain or gluten-free)
- 1/2 cup tomato sauce
- 1 cup mixed vegetables (mushrooms, bell peppers, onions)
- 1 cup vegan cheese
- Italian seasoning, to taste

Instructions

1. **Preheat Oven:**
    - Preheat your oven according to the pizza crust instructions.
2. **Assemble Pizza:**
    - Spread tomato sauce over the crust, top with vegetables and vegan cheese. Sprinkle with Italian seasoning.
3. **Bake:**
    - Bake according to crust instructions, usually about 10-15 minutes.
4. **Serve:**
    - Slice and enjoy hot!

Lentil and Quinoa Salad

Ingredients

- 1 cup cooked lentils
- 1 cup cooked quinoa
- 1 cup cherry tomatoes, halved
- 1 cucumber, diced
- 1/4 red onion, diced
- 2 tablespoons olive oil
- Juice of 1 lemon
- Salt and pepper, to taste

Instructions

1. **Combine Ingredients:**
    - In a large bowl, mix cooked lentils, quinoa, cherry tomatoes, cucumber, and red onion.
2. **Dress Salad:**
    - Drizzle with olive oil and lemon juice, then season with salt and pepper.
3. **Serve:**
    - Toss gently and enjoy!

Raw Veggie Spring Rolls

Ingredients

- Rice paper wrappers
- 1 cup mixed veggies (carrots, cucumber, bell peppers)
- Fresh herbs (mint, basil)
- Dipping sauce (soy sauce, peanut sauce, or hoisin)

Instructions

1. **Soak Wrappers:**
    - Dip rice paper wrappers in warm water until soft, about 10-15 seconds.
2. **Fill Rolls:**
    - Layer mixed veggies and herbs in the center of each wrapper. Fold the sides in and roll tightly.
3. **Serve:**
    - Serve with your choice of dipping sauce!

Tomato Basil Gazpacho

Ingredients

- 4 ripe tomatoes, chopped
- 1 cucumber, peeled and diced
- 1 bell pepper, chopped
- 1/4 red onion, chopped
- 2 cloves garlic, minced
- 1/4 cup fresh basil, chopped
- 2 tablespoons olive oil
- Salt and pepper, to taste
- 1 tablespoon red wine vinegar

Instructions

1. **Blend Ingredients:**
   - In a blender, combine tomatoes, cucumber, bell pepper, onion, garlic, basil, olive oil, salt, pepper, and vinegar. Blend until smooth.
2. **Chill:**
   - Refrigerate for at least 30 minutes to allow flavors to meld.
3. **Serve:**
   - Enjoy chilled as a refreshing soup!

Banana Oatmeal Cookies

Ingredients

- 2 ripe bananas, mashed
- 1 cup rolled oats
- 1/2 teaspoon cinnamon
- 1/4 cup dark chocolate chips (optional)

Instructions

1. **Preheat Oven:**
   - Preheat oven to 350°F (175°C) and line a baking sheet with parchment paper.
2. **Mix Ingredients:**
   - In a bowl, combine mashed bananas, oats, cinnamon, and chocolate chips if using.
3. **Scoop Cookies:**
   - Drop spoonfuls of the mixture onto the prepared baking sheet.
4. **Bake:**
   - Bake for 10-12 minutes until lightly golden.
5. **Serve:**
   - Let cool slightly before enjoying!

Enjoy these easy and delicious recipes!

Chickpea and Spinach Stew

Ingredients

- 1 can chickpeas, drained and rinsed
- 2 cups fresh spinach
- 1 onion, chopped
- 2 cloves garlic, minced
- 1 can diced tomatoes
- 1 teaspoon cumin
- Salt and pepper, to taste
- Olive oil, for sautéing

Instructions

1. **Sauté Onions and Garlic:**
    - In a pot, heat olive oil over medium heat. Add onion and garlic, cooking until soft.
2. **Add Tomatoes and Spices:**
    - Stir in diced tomatoes, chickpeas, cumin, salt, and pepper. Simmer for 10 minutes.
3. **Add Spinach:**
    - Fold in spinach and cook until wilted.
4. **Serve:**
    - Enjoy hot with crusty bread or over rice!

Vegan Tofu Scramble

Ingredients

- 1 block firm tofu, drained and crumbled
- 1/2 cup bell pepper, diced
- 1/2 cup onion, diced
- 2 cloves garlic, minced
- 1 teaspoon turmeric
- Salt and pepper, to taste
- Olive oil, for sautéing
- Fresh herbs, for garnish (optional)

Instructions

1. **Sauté Vegetables:**
    - In a skillet, heat olive oil over medium heat. Add bell pepper, onion, and garlic, sautéing until soft.
2. **Add Tofu and Seasonings:**
    - Add crumbled tofu, turmeric, salt, and pepper. Cook for 5-7 minutes, stirring occasionally.
3. **Serve:**
    - Garnish with fresh herbs if desired and enjoy!

Black Bean and Corn Salad

Ingredients

- 1 can black beans, drained and rinsed
- 1 cup corn (fresh or frozen)
- 1 bell pepper, diced
- 1/4 red onion, diced
- Juice of 1 lime
- 1 tablespoon olive oil
- Salt and pepper, to taste
- Cilantro, for garnish (optional)

Instructions

1. **Combine Ingredients:**
   - In a large bowl, mix black beans, corn, bell pepper, and red onion.
2. **Dress Salad:**
   - Drizzle with lime juice, olive oil, salt, and pepper. Toss to combine.
3. **Serve:**
   - Garnish with cilantro if desired and enjoy!

Smashed Chickpea Salad

Ingredients

- 1 can chickpeas, drained and rinsed
- 1/4 cup vegan mayonnaise
- 1 tablespoon Dijon mustard
- 1 celery stalk, diced
- 1/4 red onion, diced
- Salt and pepper, to taste
- Lettuce or bread, for serving

Instructions

1. **Mash Chickpeas:**
   - In a bowl, mash chickpeas with a fork until chunky.
2. **Mix Ingredients:**
   - Stir in vegan mayonnaise, Dijon mustard, celery, red onion, salt, and pepper.
3. **Serve:**
   - Serve on lettuce leaves or as a sandwich filling!

Quick Vegetable Curry

Ingredients

- 2 cups mixed vegetables (carrots, peas, bell peppers)
- 1 can coconut milk
- 2 tablespoons curry powder
- Salt and pepper, to taste
- Olive oil, for sautéing

Instructions

1. **Sauté Vegetables:**
    - In a pot, heat olive oil over medium heat. Add mixed vegetables and cook for 5 minutes.
2. **Add Coconut Milk and Curry Powder:**
    - Stir in coconut milk, curry powder, salt, and pepper. Simmer for 10 minutes.
3. **Serve:**
    - Enjoy over rice or with naan!

Pasta Salad with Cherry Tomatoes

Ingredients

- 8 oz pasta (your choice)
- 1 cup cherry tomatoes, halved
- 1/2 cucumber, diced
- 1/4 cup olives, sliced
- 2 tablespoons olive oil
- 1 tablespoon balsamic vinegar
- Salt and pepper, to taste

Instructions

1. **Cook Pasta:**
   - Cook pasta according to package instructions. Drain and cool.
2. **Combine Ingredients:**
   - In a large bowl, mix pasta, cherry tomatoes, cucumber, and olives.
3. **Dress Salad:**
   - Drizzle with olive oil, balsamic vinegar, salt, and pepper. Toss to combine.
4. **Serve:**
   - Enjoy chilled or at room temperature!

Sweet Potato and Kale Hash

Ingredients

- 2 medium sweet potatoes, peeled and diced
- 2 cups kale, chopped
- 1 onion, diced
- 2 cloves garlic, minced
- Olive oil, for sautéing
- Salt and pepper, to taste

Instructions

1. **Cook Sweet Potatoes:**
    - In a skillet, heat olive oil over medium heat. Add sweet potatoes and cook until tender, about 10-15 minutes.
2. **Add Onion and Garlic:**
    - Stir in onion and garlic, cooking until onion is soft.
3. **Add Kale:**
    - Fold in kale and cook until wilted. Season with salt and pepper.
4. **Serve:**
    - Enjoy warm as a hearty meal!

Enjoy these delicious and nutritious recipes!

Spinach and Mushroom Wraps

Ingredients

- 4 whole grain tortillas
- 2 cups fresh spinach
- 1 cup mushrooms, sliced
- 1/2 onion, sliced
- 2 cloves garlic, minced
- 1 tablespoon olive oil
- Salt and pepper, to taste
- Vegan cream cheese or hummus (optional)

Instructions

1. **Sauté Vegetables:**
   - In a skillet, heat olive oil over medium heat. Add garlic, onion, and mushrooms, cooking until soft. Stir in spinach until wilted. Season with salt and pepper.
2. **Assemble Wraps:**
   - Spread vegan cream cheese or hummus on tortillas if using. Fill each tortilla with the sautéed mixture.
3. **Roll and Serve:**
   - Roll up tightly and slice in half. Enjoy!

Berry Smoothie Bowl

Ingredients

- 1 cup frozen mixed berries
- 1 banana
- 1 cup almond milk (or any plant-based milk)
- Toppings: granola, fresh berries, coconut flakes, nuts

Instructions

1. **Blend Smoothie:**
    - In a blender, combine frozen berries, banana, and almond milk. Blend until smooth.
2. **Serve:**
    - Pour into a bowl and top with your choice of granola, fresh berries, coconut flakes, and nuts.

Grilled Vegetable Sandwich

Ingredients

- 1 zucchini, sliced
- 1 bell pepper, sliced
- 1 eggplant, sliced
- 1 tablespoon olive oil
- Salt and pepper, to taste
- 4 slices whole grain bread
- Vegan pesto or hummus (optional)

Instructions

1. **Grill Vegetables:**
    - Preheat a grill or grill pan. Toss vegetables with olive oil, salt, and pepper. Grill until tender.
2. **Assemble Sandwich:**
    - Spread vegan pesto or hummus on bread slices. Layer grilled vegetables between two slices.
3. **Serve:**
    - Cut in half and enjoy warm!

Quinoa and Black Bean Burgers

Ingredients

- 1 cup cooked quinoa
- 1 can black beans, drained and rinsed
- 1/2 cup breadcrumbs
- 1/4 onion, diced
- 1 teaspoon cumin
- Salt and pepper, to taste
- Olive oil, for frying

Instructions

1. **Mix Ingredients:**
   - In a bowl, mash black beans and mix with quinoa, breadcrumbs, onion, cumin, salt, and pepper.
2. **Form Patties:**
   - Shape the mixture into patties.
3. **Cook Burgers:**
   - In a skillet, heat olive oil over medium heat. Cook patties for 5-6 minutes on each side until golden.
4. **Serve:**
   - Enjoy on buns or alone with toppings!

Spicy Sriracha Chickpeas

Ingredients

- 1 can chickpeas, drained and rinsed
- 1 tablespoon olive oil
- 1 tablespoon sriracha
- 1 teaspoon garlic powder
- Salt, to taste

Instructions

1. **Preheat Oven:**
   - Preheat oven to 400°F (200°C).
2. **Toss Chickpeas:**
   - In a bowl, combine chickpeas with olive oil, sriracha, garlic powder, and salt.
3. **Roast:**
   - Spread chickpeas on a baking sheet and roast for 25-30 minutes until crispy.
4. **Serve:**
   - Enjoy as a snack or salad topping!

Cabbage and Carrot Slaw

Ingredients

- 2 cups green cabbage, shredded
- 1 cup carrots, grated
- 1/4 cup apple cider vinegar
- 1 tablespoon maple syrup
- Salt and pepper, to taste

Instructions

1. **Combine Vegetables:**
    - In a bowl, mix shredded cabbage and grated carrots.
2. **Make Dressing:**
    - In a separate bowl, whisk together apple cider vinegar, maple syrup, salt, and pepper.
3. **Toss Slaw:**
    - Pour dressing over the cabbage and carrots, tossing to combine.
4. **Serve:**
    - Enjoy chilled as a side dish!

Vegan Cauliflower Buffalo Wings

Ingredients

- 1 head cauliflower, cut into florets
- 1 cup flour (any type)
- 1 cup plant-based milk
- 1 cup breadcrumbs
- 1/2 cup buffalo sauce
- Olive oil, for baking

Instructions

1. **Preheat Oven:**
   - Preheat oven to 450°F (230°C) and line a baking sheet.
2. **Prepare Coating:**
   - In a bowl, mix flour and plant-based milk to create a batter. Dip cauliflower florets in the batter, then coat in breadcrumbs.
3. **Bake:**
   - Place florets on the baking sheet and drizzle with olive oil. Bake for 20-25 minutes until golden.
4. **Add Sauce:**
   - Toss baked wings in buffalo sauce and bake for an additional 5 minutes.
5. **Serve:**
   - Enjoy with vegan ranch dressing!

Almond Butter Energy Bites

Ingredients

- 1 cup oats
- 1/2 cup almond butter
- 1/4 cup honey or maple syrup
- 1/4 cup chocolate chips (optional)
- 1/4 cup chia seeds (optional)

Instructions

1. **Mix Ingredients:**
    - In a bowl, combine oats, almond butter, honey, chocolate chips, and chia seeds. Mix until well combined.
2. **Form Bites:**
    - Roll mixture into small balls and place on a baking sheet.
3. **Chill:**
    - Refrigerate for at least 30 minutes to set.
4. **Serve:**
    - Enjoy as a quick snack or on-the-go energy boost!

Enjoy these delicious and nutritious recipes!

Simple Vegan Chili Rellenos

Ingredients

- 4 large poblano peppers
- 1 cup quinoa, cooked
- 1 can black beans, drained and rinsed
- 1 cup corn (fresh or frozen)
- 1 teaspoon cumin
- Salt and pepper, to taste
- Olive oil, for drizzling
- Vegan cheese (optional)

Instructions

1. **Preheat Oven:**
   - Preheat oven to 375°F (190°C).
2. **Prepare Peppers:**
   - Roast the poblano peppers until charred. Place them in a bowl covered with plastic wrap for 10 minutes, then peel off the skin.
3. **Mix Filling:**
   - In a bowl, combine cooked quinoa, black beans, corn, cumin, salt, and pepper.
4. **Stuff Peppers:**
   - Carefully stuff the roasted peppers with the quinoa mixture. Place them in a baking dish and drizzle with olive oil.
5. **Bake:**
   - Bake for 20-25 minutes. If using, sprinkle vegan cheese on top in the last 5 minutes.
6. **Serve:**
   - Enjoy warm!

Rice and Bean Bowl

Ingredients

- 1 cup cooked rice (brown or white)
- 1 can black beans, drained and rinsed
- 1 cup corn
- 1/2 avocado, sliced
- 1/4 cup salsa
- Fresh cilantro, for garnish
- Lime wedges, for serving

Instructions

1. **Combine Ingredients:**
    - In a bowl, layer cooked rice, black beans, corn, and avocado.
2. **Add Salsa:**
    - Top with salsa and garnish with fresh cilantro.
3. **Serve:**
    - Squeeze lime juice over the bowl and enjoy!

Zesty Lemon Couscous Salad

Ingredients

- 1 cup couscous
- 1 1/4 cups vegetable broth
- 1 cup cherry tomatoes, halved
- 1 cucumber, diced
- 1/4 red onion, diced
- Juice of 1 lemon
- 2 tablespoons olive oil
- Salt and pepper, to taste

Instructions

1. **Cook Couscous:**
    - In a saucepan, bring vegetable broth to a boil. Stir in couscous, cover, and remove from heat. Let sit for 5 minutes, then fluff with a fork.
2. **Combine Salad Ingredients:**
    - In a large bowl, mix cooked couscous, cherry tomatoes, cucumber, and red onion.
3. **Dress Salad:**
    - Drizzle with lemon juice, olive oil, salt, and pepper. Toss to combine.
4. **Serve:**
    - Enjoy chilled or at room temperature!

Chickpea and Avocado Dip

Ingredients

- 1 can chickpeas, drained and rinsed
- 1 ripe avocado
- 1 tablespoon lemon juice
- 1 clove garlic, minced
- Salt and pepper, to taste
- Olive oil, for drizzling

Instructions

1. **Mash Ingredients:**
    - In a bowl, mash chickpeas and avocado together.
2. **Add Seasonings:**
    - Stir in lemon juice, garlic, salt, and pepper. Adjust seasoning to taste.
3. **Serve:**
    - Drizzle with olive oil and enjoy with pita chips or veggies!

Vegan Burrito Bowl

Ingredients

- 1 cup cooked brown rice
- 1 can black beans, drained and rinsed
- 1 cup corn
- 1 avocado, diced
- 1/2 cup salsa
- 1/4 cup chopped cilantro

Instructions

1. **Layer Ingredients:**
    - In a bowl, layer cooked brown rice, black beans, corn, avocado, and salsa.
2. **Garnish:**
    - Top with chopped cilantro.
3. **Serve:**
    - Enjoy as a filling meal!

Coconut Curry Noodles

Ingredients

- 8 oz rice noodles
- 1 can coconut milk
- 2 tablespoons curry paste
- 2 cups mixed vegetables (bell peppers, broccoli, snap peas)
- Fresh cilantro, for garnish
- Lime wedges, for serving

Instructions

1. **Cook Noodles:**
   - Cook rice noodles according to package instructions. Drain and set aside.
2. **Make Sauce:**
   - In a large pan, heat coconut milk and curry paste over medium heat. Stir until combined.
3. **Add Vegetables:**
   - Add mixed vegetables and cook until tender.
4. **Combine:**
   - Toss cooked noodles with the curry sauce and vegetables.
5. **Serve:**
   - Garnish with fresh cilantro and serve with lime wedges.

Cucumber and Avocado Salad

Ingredients

- 1 cucumber, diced
- 1 avocado, diced
- 1/4 red onion, thinly sliced
- Juice of 1 lime
- Salt and pepper, to taste
- Fresh dill or cilantro, for garnish (optional)

Instructions

1. **Combine Salad Ingredients:**
   - In a bowl, mix diced cucumber, avocado, and red onion.
2. **Dress Salad:**
   - Drizzle with lime juice, and season with salt and pepper. Toss gently.
3. **Serve:**
   - Garnish with fresh dill or cilantro if desired, and enjoy!

Quick Veggie Tacos

Ingredients

- 8 small corn tortillas
- 1 cup mixed vegetables (zucchini, bell peppers, onions)
- 1 can black beans, drained and rinsed
- 1 avocado, sliced
- Fresh cilantro, for garnish
- Lime wedges, for serving

Instructions

1. **Sauté Vegetables:**
    - In a skillet, cook mixed vegetables over medium heat until tender.
2. **Warm Tortillas:**
    - Warm corn tortillas in a separate skillet or microwave.
3. **Assemble Tacos:**
    - Fill each tortilla with sautéed vegetables, black beans, and avocado.
4. **Serve:**
    - Garnish with fresh cilantro and serve with lime wedges!

Enjoy these flavorful and nutritious recipes!

Lemon Garlic Quinoa

Ingredients

- 1 cup quinoa
- 2 cups vegetable broth or water
- 2 tablespoons olive oil
- 2 cloves garlic, minced
- Juice of 1 lemon
- Salt and pepper, to taste
- Fresh parsley, chopped (for garnish)

Instructions

1. **Cook Quinoa:**
    - Rinse quinoa under cold water. In a saucepan, combine quinoa and vegetable broth. Bring to a boil, then reduce heat, cover, and simmer for 15 minutes or until liquid is absorbed.
2. **Sauté Garlic:**
    - In a small pan, heat olive oil over medium heat. Add minced garlic and sauté for 1-2 minutes until fragrant.
3. **Combine Ingredients:**
    - Fluff the cooked quinoa with a fork, then stir in the sautéed garlic, lemon juice, salt, and pepper.
4. **Serve:**
    - Garnish with fresh parsley and enjoy!

Sweet Potato and Chickpea Buddha Bowl

Ingredients

- 1 large sweet potato, diced
- 1 can chickpeas, drained and rinsed
- 2 tablespoons olive oil
- 1 teaspoon paprika
- Salt and pepper, to taste
- 2 cups kale, chopped
- 1 avocado, sliced
- Tahini or your favorite dressing (for drizzling)

Instructions

1. **Preheat Oven:**
    - Preheat oven to 400°F (200°C).
2. **Roast Sweet Potato and Chickpeas:**
    - Toss sweet potato and chickpeas with olive oil, paprika, salt, and pepper. Spread on a baking sheet and roast for 25-30 minutes until tender.
3. **Prepare Kale:**
    - While roasting, massage chopped kale with a little olive oil and salt to soften.
4. **Assemble Bowl:**
    - In a bowl, layer kale, roasted sweet potato, chickpeas, and avocado.
5. **Serve:**
    - Drizzle with tahini or your favorite dressing and enjoy!

Vegan Apple Crisp

Ingredients

- 4 cups apples, peeled and sliced
- 1 tablespoon lemon juice
- 1/2 cup oats
- 1/2 cup flour (whole wheat or gluten-free)
- 1/2 cup brown sugar
- 1 teaspoon cinnamon
- 1/4 cup coconut oil or vegan butter, melted

Instructions

1. **Preheat Oven:**
   - Preheat oven to 350°F (175°C).
2. **Prepare Apples:**
   - In a bowl, toss sliced apples with lemon juice. Place in a greased baking dish.
3. **Make Crisp Topping:**
   - In a separate bowl, mix oats, flour, brown sugar, cinnamon, and melted coconut oil until crumbly.
4. **Assemble and Bake:**
   - Sprinkle the crisp topping over the apples and bake for 30-35 minutes until golden and bubbly.
5. **Serve:**
   - Enjoy warm, optionally with vegan ice cream!

No-Bake Chocolate Energy Bars

Ingredients

- 1 cup dates, pitted
- 1 cup nuts (almonds, walnuts, or pecans)
- 1/2 cup cocoa powder
- 1/4 cup almond butter or peanut butter
- 1/4 cup maple syrup or honey
- 1/4 cup dark chocolate chips (optional)

Instructions

1. **Blend Ingredients:**
    - In a food processor, combine dates, nuts, cocoa powder, almond butter, and maple syrup. Blend until a sticky dough forms.
2. **Add Chocolate Chips:**
    - If using, fold in dark chocolate chips.
3. **Press into Pan:**
    - Line a small baking dish with parchment paper. Press the mixture firmly into the dish.
4. **Chill:**
    - Refrigerate for at least 1 hour to set.
5. **Cut and Serve:**
    - Cut into bars and enjoy as a quick snack!

Enjoy these delicious and nutritious recipes!